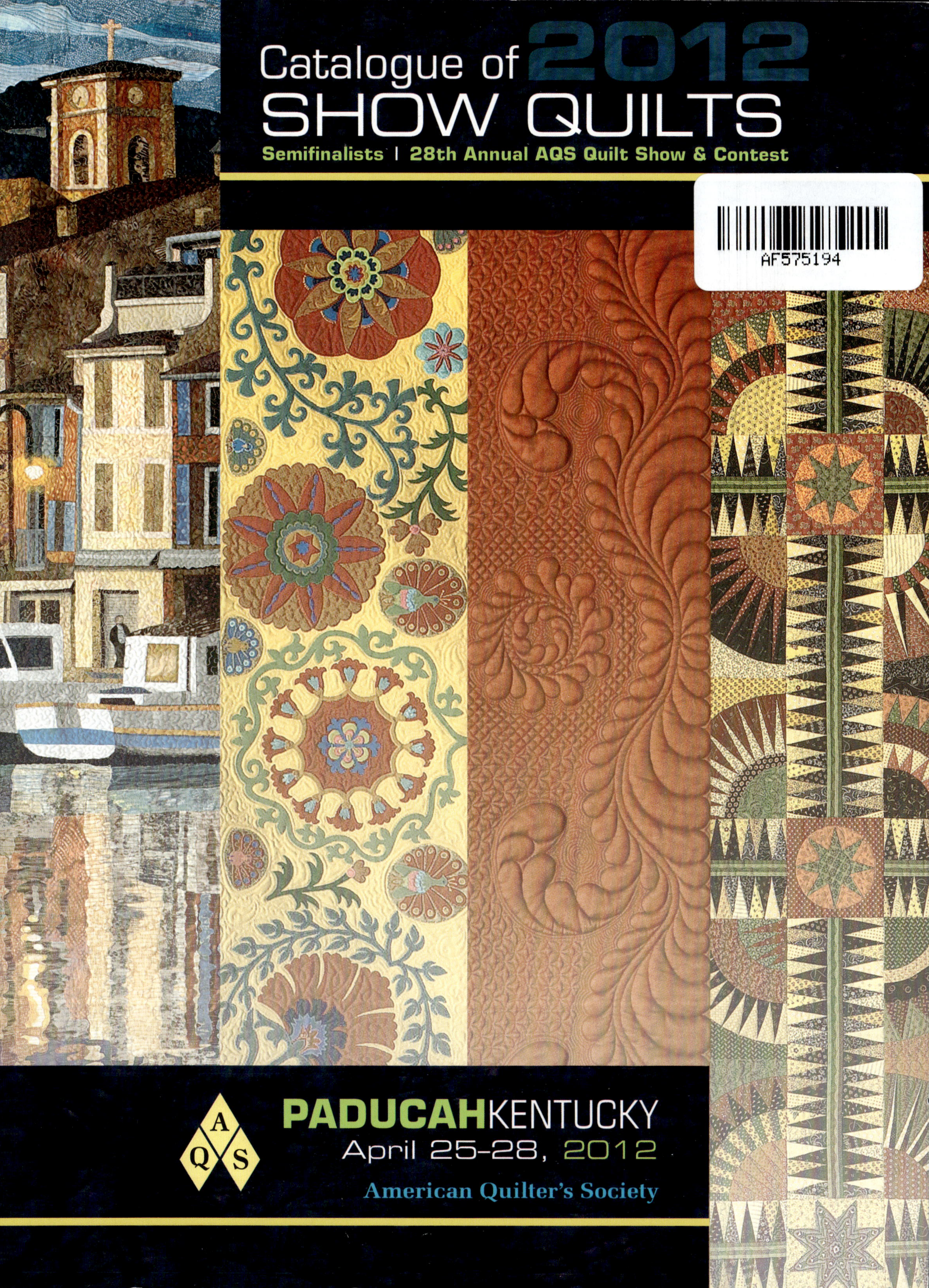

Catalogue of 2012 SHOW QUILTS

Semifinalists | 28th Annual AQS Quilt Show & Contest

AQS

PADUCAH KENTUCKY

April 25-28, 2012

American Quilter's Society

Located in Paducah, Kentucky, the American Quilter's Society (AQS) is dedicated to promoting the accomplishments of today's quilters. Through its publications and events, AQS strives to honor today's quiltmakers and their work and to inspire future creativity and innovation in quiltmaking.

Executive Editor: Andi Milam Reynolds
Editor: Bonnie K. Browning
Graphic Design: Elaine Wilson
Cover Design: Michael Buckingham
Photography: Supplied by the individual quiltmakers

Additional copies of this book may be ordered from the American Quilter's Society, PO Box 3290, Paducah, KY 42002-3290, or online at www.AmericanQuilter.com.

Cover, title page, and details: Port of Cassis, 52" x 48", Lenore Crawford, Midland, MI. Paisley Peacock, 60" x 72", Pat Holly, Ann Arbor, MI. Five Bar Blues, 50" x 64", Diane Loomis, Sudbury, MA. New York Jazz, 74" x 74", Patricia T. Mayer and Karen Watts, Houston, TX.

Proudly printed and bound in the United States of America

The 28th Annual AQS Quilt Show & Contest is April 25 – 28, 2012. More than $120,000 will be awarded to the winners of this year's contest, with the Janome Best of Show winner receiving $20,000. More than 500 quilts will be on display.

Quilters from 45 U.S. states and 11 countries entered their quilts this year. Techniques in the 377 quilts in the contest range from traditional piecing and appliqué, quilting by hand and machine, to innovative use of embroidery, painting, crystals, Zentangle®, and other embellishments.

Enter your quilts in the 2013 AQS Quilt Show & Contest – you could be the next big winner!

Meredith Schroeder

Meredith Schroeder
AQS President and Founder

CATEGORY NUMBERS | CATEGORY

Baltimore Beauties & Beyond: Studies in Classic Album Quilt Appliqué, Vol I by Elly Sienkiewicz, C&T Publishing, ©1995; *The Best of Baltimore Beauties Part II: More Patterns for Album Blocks*, by Elly Sienkiewicz, C&T Publishing, ©2002

101. Challenge 2, 82"x 82"
Georgina Buschauer, Houston, TX

Barbara Brackman's Encyclopedia of Appliqué: 2000 Traditional and Modern Designs, Updated History of Appliqué: New! 5 Quilt Projects by Barbara Brackman, C&T Publications, ©2009

102. Symphony of Roses, 87" x 87"
Barbara Clem, Rockford, IL

103. Stars in My Life, 71" x 92"
Linda Kay Gapp, Lincoln, NE

104. Baltimore Garden in the Round
89" x 90", Treva Gurley, Ada, OK

Artful Album Quilts: Appliqué Inspirations from Traditional Blocks by Jane Townswick, Martingale and Company, ©2001; *Color-Blend Appliqué* by Jane Townswick, That Patchwork Place, Martingale and Company, ©2011; *The Best of Baltimore Beauties* by Elly Sienkiewicz, C&T Publishing, ©2000; *Baltimore Beauties and Beyond: Studies in Classic Album Quilt Appliqué, Vol. I* by Elly Sienkiewicz, C&T Publishing, ©1995. Inspired by a workshop with Jane Townswick.

Victorian Calling Cards pattern, Jenifer Buechel Ornamental Appliqué

105. Eternity, 77" x 87"
Kyoko Hata and Yukiko Hirano
Yokohama, Kanagawa, Japan

106. Victorian Friendship Calling Card
71" x 82", Patricia Hobbs, Macomb, IL

107. Beautiful Sunset, 83" x 95"
Kaoru Ito, Meguro, Tokyo, Japan

108. Kirara's Walking Road in the Wood, 89" x 84"
Ayako Kawakami, Funabashi, Chiba, Japan

Design by Kathy Nakajima

109. Flowers in My Heart, 89" x 89"
Noriko Kido, Azumino, Nagano, Japan

Inspired by two quilts made by Mary Brown of East Nottingham, MD in the 1850's

110. Sam's Owl (A Mary Brown Album)
104" x 101", Barbara Korengold
Chevy Chase, MD

111. Harmony, 68" x 81"
Masako Kotaki, Yotsukaido, Chiba, Japan

112. Decade 2001 - 2011, 90" x 90"
Gillian Lee, St.-Sauveur, Quebec, Canada

Papercuts and Plenty: Volume Three of Baltimore Beauties and Beyond by Elly Sienkiewicz, C&T Publishing, ©1995; Feathered Star workshop by Rosemary Makham

113. Stars on a Bed of Feathers
83" x 83", Pamela Mann, Elliston, VA

114. Enchanted Garden, 81" x 81"
Cathleen Miller, Albuquerque, NM

115. Jazz, 71" x 83"
Megumi Mizuno, Shiki, Saitama, Japan

116. May Baskets, 81" x 81"
Hallie H. O'Kelley, Tuscaloosa, AL

Summers' End block #9 by Maggie Walker Design, ©2000

117. Fruit and Feathers, 84" x 84"
Marie O'Kelley, Seattle, WA

Roseville Album pattern by Kim McLean, GloriousColor.com

118. The Bizzy Bird Farm, 91" x 91"
Julee Prose, Ottumwa, IA

119. Multi Fan Star, 98" x 112"
Joyce Puffinbarger, Symsonia, KY

Multi Fan Star pattern, *In Love with Log Cabins* by Nancy Fitzpatrick, Oxmoor House, ©1995

120. Midnight Rendezvous, 84" x 84"
Barbara Shiffler, Statesboro, GA

Butterfly 2 from *Fantastic Fans: Exquisite Quilts and Other Projects,* by Alice Dunsdon, C&T Publishing, ©2003; *Turkish Delights to Appliqué* by Linda M. Poole, American Quilter's Society, ©2002

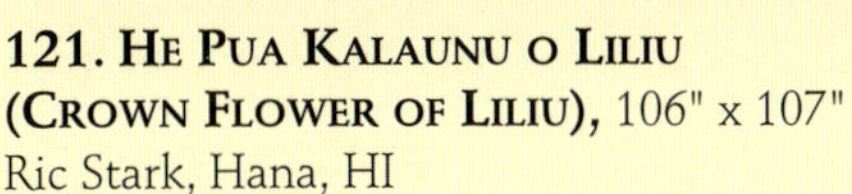

121. He Pua Kalaunu o Liliu (Crown Flower of Liliu), 106" x 107"
Ric Stark, Hana, HI

122. Vitamin Quilt, 82" x 84"
Hiromi Suzuki, Meguro, Tokyo, Japan

123. Arrangement, 81" x 81"
Fusako Takido, Shizuoka, Shizuoka, Japan

124. Anniversary, 80" x 80",
Kyouko Tashiro
Shirakawa, Fukushima, Japan

Design by Keiko Miyauchi

The Best of Baltimore Beauties, Part II. More Patterns for Album Blocks by Elly Sienkiewicz, C&T Publishing, ©2002

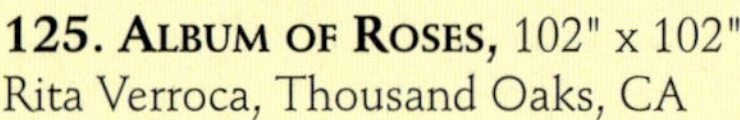

125. Album of Roses, 102" x 102"
Rita Verroca, Thousand Oaks, CA

126. Bolero 21609, 88" x 101"
Isako Wada, Kurokawa, Miyagi, Japan

Design inspired by British-American quilter Albert Small

127. Scarborough Fowle, 81" x 81"
Mary Abott Williams, Pinehurst, NC

Scarborough Faire/Rainbow Hill project, *Classic English Medallion Style Quilts* by Bettina Havig, American Quilter's Society, ©2003

128. Angel's Trumpet Flower
91" x 95", Mie Yamada,
Setagaya, Tokyo, Japan

201. Turkish Delight, 86" x 86"
Helen Williams Butler, Alpine, UT

Star of Bethlehem pattern by Edyta Sitar of Laundry Basket Quilts

202. Star of Bethlehem, 85" x 85"
Janet Davis, Alamosa, CO

203. Tibetan Mandala: For Wisdom and Compassion, 83" x 86"
Barbara E. Lies, Madison, WI

Golden fish motif from *The Encyclopedia of Tibetan Symbols and Motifs* by Robert Beer, Boston, 1999. Reprinted by arrangement with Shambhala Publications, Inc., Boston, MA.

204. Acanthus with a Twist
89" x 99", Mary E. Olson
Aumsville, OR

205. Christmas Waltz, 84" x 84"
Loretta Painter, Norris, TN

206. Trellis of Roses, 80" x 98"
Sophie M. Pelletier, Meriden, CT

Pattern from *Garden Twist Quilts from In the Beginning Fabrics* by Sharon Yenter, In The Beginning, ©2007

207. Amethyst Fanflowers, 82" x 82"
Laurie Schoenebeck, Mountain, WI

208. Luminous Stars, 84" x 84"
Mildred Sorrells, Macomb, IL

Summertime pattern designed by Erica Kaprow

301. A Year of Summertime, 73" x 93"
Sonia Blue, Fayetteville, NC

Inspired by a Strip and Slash workshop by Jackie Robinson

302. A Trove of Triangles
93" x 93", SuEllen Brauer, Decatur, IL

303. Swirling Parasols, 106"x 106"
Christine Clark, Eufaula, OK

Japanese Fan pattern by Judy Niemeyer

304. Granddaughters' Flower Garden, 64" x 81"
Jan Cunningham, Acworth, GA

Aunt Millie's Garden: 12 Flowering Blocks from Piece O' Cake Designs by Becky Goldsmith and Linda Jenkins, C&T Publishing, ©2007

Galaxy of Stars pattern by Lynn Dash

305. Millenium Stars, 85" x 85"
Cindy Erickson, Papillion, NE

Picket Fence pattern, *String Quilts: 10 Fun Patterns for Innovating and Renovating* by Elsie M. Campbell, ©2009 GoodBooks (www.GoodBooks.com)

306. Folded Fans, 82" x 99"
Dorinda Evans, Madison, MS

307. Elsa's Knot, 87" x 87"
Ann Helbling, Kindred, ND

Solar Flare project from *Blocks to Diamonds: Kaleidoscope Star Quilts from Traditional Blocks* by Cheryl Malkowski, C&T Publishing, ©2010

308. Garden Nouveau, 80" x 100"
Judy Humphrey, Lonedell, MO

Garden Nouveau Quilts by Vicky Lawrence, American Quilter's Society, ©2009

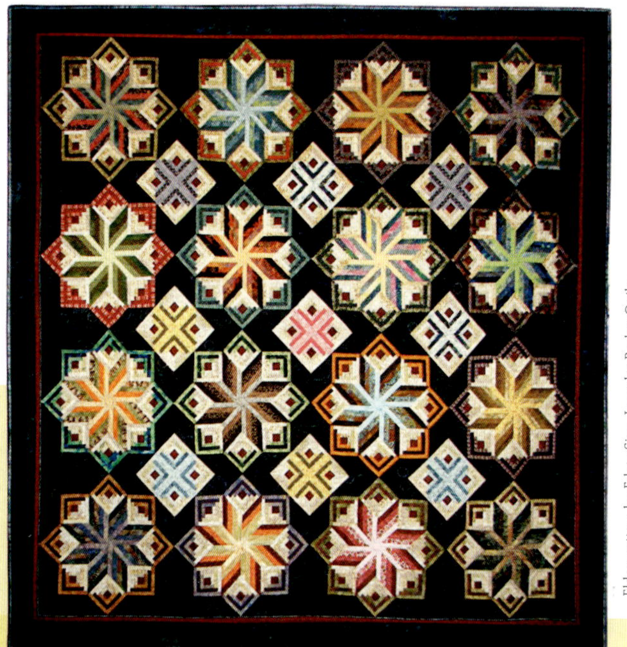

Eldon pattern by Edyta Sitar, Laundry Basket Quilts

309. Persistence, 86" x 86"
Karen Kielmeyer, Bella Vista, AR

310. Logs & Stars in Scraps
86" x 86", Leslie Kiger
Saint Simons Island, GA

311. Radiant Strips, 75" x 95"
Patricia C. Kilmark, Atlanta, GA

312. Homage to Mary Brown: Patience Rewarded, 97" x 97"
Audrey Manning, Exelsior, MN

Tribute to Mary Brown pattern, Patricia Cox, One of a Kind Quilting Designs

313. CRIMSON RADIANCE, 91" x 91"
Charlotte McRanie and Shannon Baker
Black Mountain, NC

314. THRU GRANDMOTHER'S WINDOW
79" x 99", Barbara Nickelson, Wichita, KS

Thru Grandmother's Window pattern ©Piece O' Cake Designs

315. SPACE WONDER, 110" x 110"
Beth Nufer and Shelley Knapp
Brookings, OR

Center inspired by VANISHING POINT by Chris Lynn Kirsch, *Quilt Art Engagement Calendar*, American Quilter's Society, ©2010

316. POTTER MARSH, 69" x 84"
Nancy Parmelee, Sonoma, CA

Inspired by traditional Goose in the Pond block

Yoyoville pattern by Bunny Hill Designs

317. Behind Closed Doors, 70" x 88"
Karolyn Reker and Denise Waymeyer
Cartersville, GA

Butterscotch Tart pattern, Fig Tree and Co.

318. Summer Breeze, 82" x 82"
Sharyl L. Schlieckau, Loganville, WI

319. Storm at Sea – Bay View
85" x 92", Sheri Schoenebeck, Wichita, KS

Any Port in a Storm quilt from *A New Light on Storm at Sea Quilts: One Block - An Ocean of Design Possibilities* by Wendy Mathson, C&T Publishing, ©2009

320. Licorice & Lace, 96" x 100"
Birgit Schueller, Riegelsberg, Germany

Bed Quilts, *Longarm / Midarm Machine Quilted*
Bed Quilts, *Group*

Hugs and Kisses pattern by Sue Garman, 2010 TQS Block of the Month

Jenny Haskins *Special Edition* design CD *Simon's Folly: A Quilt by Simon Haskins*

321. Hugs and Kisses, 69" x 85"
Gail H. Smith, Barrington, IL

322. Charlotte, 95" x 95"
Charlotte Wright and Jessica Schick
Stillwater, OK

401. 13-Year President's Quilt
87" x 101", Camelia Elliott, Pilot, VA

402. Abo Canyon Memories
65" x 91", Gail Garber, Donna Barnitz, and Michele Hymel, Albuquerque, NM

403. Ms. MacDonald Had a Farm,
83" x 86", Hanging By a Thread
Chehalis, WA

Original pattern by Kathy Nakajima

404. Remember The Tahiti
91" x 91", Shigeko Haruki & 8 Friends
Setagaya, Tokyo, Japan

405. Nine Patch Goose Chase, 90" x 90"
Colleen Henrichs, Osceola, IA

Based on an antique quilt at the Quilt Study Center & Museum, Lincoln, NE

406. Following the Curves,
97" x 97", Toby Lischko, Dolores Keaton,
and Terri Kanyuck, Beaufort, MO

Inspired by the 2003 *Times and Seasons Calendar* "Heart of America" pattern by Piecemakers Country Store

407. Indiana Barns, 83" x 97"
Dinah Miller, North Salem, IN

408. Celtic Lullaby, 95" x 95"
Jan Ochterbeck, St Louis, MO

409. Autumn in the Ozarks, 95" x 95"
Ozark Piecemakers Guild, Springfield, MO

410. Red Stars at Night 3 Quilters Delight, 68" x 88", Loretta Painter, Cyndi Herrmann, and Kate Meyers, Norris, TN

Appliqué Affair, Edyta Sitar, Laundry Basket Quilts

411. AUTUMN SPLENDOR, 84" x 84"
Prairie Quilt Guild, Sedgwick, KS

412. CELESTIAL GARDEN, 82" x 82"
Prairie Star Quilters Guild, Wayne, IL

413. GOLDEN RADIANCE, 110" x 110"
Riverwalk Quilters Guild, Naperville, IL

414. DEAR FRIENDS, 91" x 91"
Michiko Yanagihara & 8 Friends
Gotemba, Shizuoka, Japan

Workshop with Keiko Miyauchi

Appliqué Designs: My Mother Taught Me to Sew by Faye Anderson, American Quilter's Society, ©2001

501. Trio of Flowers, 78" x 78"
Hisae Abe, Katsusikaku, Tokyo, Japan

502. April Garden, 76" x 88"
Kim Me Ae, Seoul, South Korea

503. Lovely Garden Part II, 78" x 78"
Tomoko Arai, Tsuruoka,Yamagata, Japan

504. The Wizard of Oz, 61" x 47"
Eleanor J. Carlson, Cadillac, MI

Based on scenes and characters from the movie *The Wizard of Oz* produced by Metro-Goldwyn-Mayer

505. Butterflies Flew to My Garden
73" x 74", Marie Anne Coadic
Wilmington, NC

506. Organic Log Cabin, 73" x 88"
Jennifer Emry, Arlington, VA

507. A Week of Anne, 67" x 76"
Naoko Esaki, Komaki, Aichi, Japan

508. Ladies of the Sea, 82" x 84"
Barbara (Bobbe) Green, Paducah, KY

Adapted from Ladies of the Sea patterns, Susan H. Garman, Quakertown Quilts

Inspired by toile fabric

509. Baltimore in the Provence
80" x 80", Ellen Heck, Somis, CA

510. Crystal World, 69" x 69"
Yuriko Ikuma
Hamamatsu, Shizuoka, Japan

511. Michishirube, 76" x 76"
Kyoko Inagaki, Osaka, Osaka, Japan

Workshop with Noriko Masui

512. A Symphony of Love, 77" x 77"
Kiyoko Ishihara, Ashikaga, Tochigi, Japan

Workshop with Noriko Masui

513. Pua O Manoa, 81" x 88"
Michiyo Kato, Tsushima, Aichi, Japan

514. Thank You Quilt, 87" x 87"
Yachiyo Katsuno
Setagaya, Tokyo, Japan

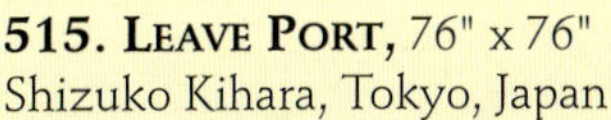

515. Leave Port, 76" x 76"
Shizuko Kihara, Tokyo, Japan

516. The Birders, 68" x 43"
Suzanne Marshall, Clayton, MO

Based on *The Humorous Dreams of Pantagruel*, a sixteenth-century manuscript by Francois Rabelais

The Elegant Floral Quilting Designs, Reiko Washizawa

517. CELEBRATE, 64" x 65"
Kazumi Matsuo, Kawabe, Hyogo, Japan

Dimensional Appliqué, Baskets, Blooms & Baltimore Borders, by Elly Sienkiewicz, C&T Publishing, ©1993; *Wildflowers: Designs for Appliqué & Quilting*, by Carol Armstrong, C&T Publishing, ©2010; *From a Quilter's Garden: A Fresh Crop of Appliqué Designs* by Gabrielle Swain, That Patchwork Place, © 1996

518. MY FAVORITE THINGS, 71" x 71"
Terrie L. Newman, Hot Springs, AR

519. FOREVER IN MY HEART, 78" x 78"
Lahala Phelps, Bonney Lake, WA

Inspired by the 1885 antique quilt BLEEDING HEART by Mary Ann Grove as seen in *A Treasury of Mennonite Quilts* by Rachel and Kenneth Pellman, ©Good Books (www.GoodBooks.com), 1992

520. TENNESSEE TREASURES, 72" x 72"
Linda M. Roy, Knoxville, TN

Workshop with Noriko Masui

Embroidery on back inspired by Sieglinde Schoen Smith

521. Ocean Blue, 75" x 75"
Noriko Sato, Chigasaki, Kanagawa, Japan

522. Star Struck, 91" x 80"
Cheryl L. See, Ashburn, VA

523. Flower Quartet, 75" x 75"
Yasuko Sugaya, Ichihara, Chiba, Japan

524. Sunlight, 75" x 75"
Akemi Sugiyama
Hamura, Tokyo, Japan

Workshop with Noriko Masui

Workshop with Noriko Masui

525. Flower Blooming in Paradise
75" x 75", Yumiko Takami
Kawasaki, Kanagawa, Japan

Workshop with Noriko Masui

526. In the Spring Wind, 68" x 81"
Kiyomi Takayanagi
Kitanagoya, Aichi, Japan

527. My Anniversary, 74" x 74"
Fumiyo Takemori, Mitaka, Tokyo, Japan

Workshop with Noriko Masui

528. Pineapple Plantation, 67" x 67"
Mariko Tomizawa
Kaminoyama, Yamagata, Japan

Workshop with Noriko Masui

Workshop with Noriko Masui

529. A Beautiful Day in May, 65" x 65"
Etsuko Uto, Kashima, Ibaraki, Japan

530. Collaboration, 69" x 69"
Keiko Yamada, Kusatsu, Shiga, Japan

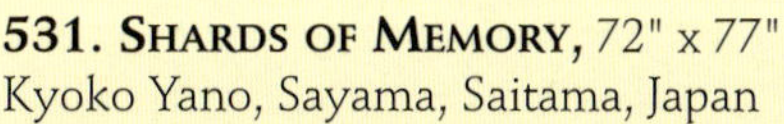

531. Shards of Memory, 72" x 77"
Kyoko Yano, Sayama, Saitama, Japan

532. Blooming with Hope
82" x 90", Junko Yazawa
Hachioji, Tokyo, Japan

601. Hearts Desire, 80" x 80"
Esther Aliu, Donvale, Victoria, Australia

602. Light Desired, 72" x 87"
Mieko Arai
Nishisirakawa, Fukushima, Japan

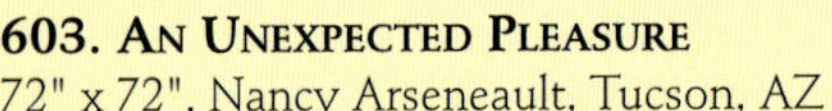

603. An Unexpected Pleasure
72" x 72", Nancy Arseneault, Tucson, AZ

Inspired by a "stash buster" class at Bella Quiltworks in Tucson, AZ

604. Reflected Symmetry, 67" x 67"
Jody Aultman, Ames, IA

Inspired by Frank Lloyd Wright stained glass windows

605. ENCHANTED BASKETS, 61"x 61"
Jean Brueggenjohan, Columbia, MO

Nine-Blade Fan project from *Fons & Porter Presents Quilts from the Henry Ford: 24 Vintage Quilts Celebrating American Quiltmaking* by Liz Porter and Marianne Fons, Landauer Corporation, www.landauercorp.com, ©2005

606. FAN FARE, 65" x 79"
Mary Chalmers, Willmar, MN

607. STONE WALL, 67"x 42"
Misun Chang, Seoul, South Korea

608. OCTOPUSSY, 76" x 62"
Janneke de Vries-Bodzinga,
Kollumerzwaag, Friesland, The Netherlands

Large Wall Quilts, *Home Machine Quilted*

Inspired by a 1930s antique quilt in the Museum of the Big Bend, Alpine, TX

Pattern Fiesta de Talavera by J. Michelle Watts from *Quilters Newsletter*, Feb/Mar issue, 2011. Pattern available from jmichellewatts.com

609. Wagon Wheel Flowers, 64" x 83"
Paula Doyle, The Woodlands, TX

610. Party Dishes – Ready to Party
70" x 70", Charmaine Erickson
Olive Branch, MS

611. Feathers in the Wind, 61" x 42"
Caryl Bryer Fallert, Paducah, KY

612. Conversations with Diane
63" x 62", Ming Hsu
Woodside, South Australia, Australia

Feathered Star Quilt Blocks I by Marsha McCloskey, Feathered Star Productions, Inc., ©2003; *Guide to Machine Quilting* by Diane Gaudynski, American Quilter's Society, ©2002, *Gaudynski's Machine Quilting Guidebook* by Diane Gaudynski, American Quilter's Society, ©2006

613. When Spring Comes, 68"x 63"
Yukiko Ishizuka
Sagamihara, Kanagawa, Japan

614. Song of the Earth, 71" x 71"
Liz Jones, Leominster,
Herefordshire, United Kingdom

615. Sad City of Survivor, 76" x 44"
Young Joo-Wi, Seoul, South Korea

616. The Garden Terrace in June
61" x 68", Masae Kashizaki
Yokohama, Kanagawa, Japan

Workshop with Yoko Ueda

617. Neuron III, 66" x 40"
Pamela Kirch, Cazenovia, NY

Sheep Wannabees pattern by Debora Konshinsky of Critter Pattern Works. Pattern available at www.critterpat.com.

618. Sheep Wannabees, 70" x 70"
Debora Konchinsky, Breinigsville, PA

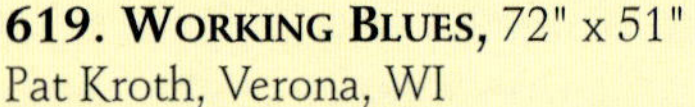

619. Working Blues, 72" x 51"
Pat Kroth, Verona, WI

620. Old China, 63" x 61"
Nita Markos, Hillsboro, IL

621. Specimens, 68" x 68"
Barbara Ann McCraw, Denton, TX

622. Stars in My Garden
68" x 88", Alice Means, Bolton, CT

Stars in the Garden: Fresh Flowers in Appliqué by Becky Goldsmith, Piece O' Cake Designs, Martingale & Company, ©1998; *Aunt Millie's Garden: 12 Flowering Blocks from Piece O' Cake Designs* by Becky Goldsmith and Linda Jenkins, C&T Publishing, ©2007

623. Quilt Tidings from Switzerland
66" x 69", Natsumi Ohara
Yokohama, Kanagawa, Japan

624. Jam Session in the Twilight
69" x 77", Taeko Okamatsu
Hino, Tokyo, Japan

It's All About Triangles from *Freddy & Gwen Collaborate Again: Freewheeling Twists on Traditional Quilt Designs* by Gwen Marston and Freddy Moran, Lark Books, ©2009

625. A Tisket, A Tasket, 67" x 67"
V'Lou Oliveira, Norman, OK

626. ....holic, 60" x 60"
Kyungsu Park, Anyang, South Korea

627. Grid Lock, 67" x 71"
Jill Robinson, Appleton, WI

628. Aunt Millie's Big Blue Garden
66" x 74", Paula Rooyakkers, Evans, GA

Aunt Millie's Garden: 12 Flowering Blocks from Piece O' Cake Designs by Becky Goldsmith & Linda Jenkins, C&T Publishing, ©2007

Embroidery designs designed and digitized by zundtdesign.com

629. Radiance, 75" x 74"
Susan Stewart, Pittsburg, KS

Circle of Life pattern © Jacqueline de Jonge, BeColourful.com

630. Circle of Life, 70" x 70"
Maggie Szafranski, Urbana, IL

631. Baltimore Roses, 70" x 70"
Diana K. Trost, Toledo, OH

632. In the Garden, 85" x 40"
Catherine L. Waltz, Fort Lauderdale, FL

Large Wall Quilts, *Home Machine Quilted*
Large Wall Quilts, *Longarm / Midarm Machine Quilted*

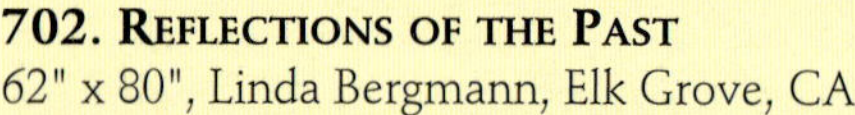

633. Norge Portals to Deep Spaces II
73" x 73", Elizabeth Whitman, Freeland, WA

Creative Expressions Special Edition: Moulin Rouge by Jenny and Simon Haskins

701. Moulin Rouge, 74" x 101"
Kenneth Berg and Joyce Ross
Port Orchard, WA

702. Reflections of the Past
62" x 80", Linda Bergmann, Elk Grove, CA

4th of July pattern by Judy and Bradley Niemeyer, Judy Niemeyer Quilting

703. Pebbles on the Path, 76" x 75"
Nancy Brieschke, Sandwich, IL

Inspired by Drunkard's Path pattern

Design inspiration from *Lovely Lane Museum 150th/50th Anniversary Quilt Patterns*, Lovely Lane Museum and Archives, Baltimore, Maryland; Crossed Laurel Sprays, Pattern 1 for Roses, and Victorian Basket patterns from *Baltimore Beauties and Beyond: Studies in Classic Album Quilt Appliqué* by Elly Sienkiewicz, C&T Publishing ©1989; Epergne of Fruit IV pattern from *Papercuts and Plenty: Studies in Classic Album Quilt Appliqué, Vol. 3* by Elly Sienkiewicz, C&T Publishing, ©1995; Metropolitan Museum Mosaic quilt pattern, *Woman's Day*, 1965; also inspired by Rober Callaham Baltimore Album Collection, RJR Fabrics

704. Pride of Baltimore II, 79" x 78"
Barbara M. Burnham and Marty Vint
Ellicott City, MD

Sidelines pattern by Debbie Bowles, Maple Island Quilts

705. Favorites, 62" x 67"
Michele Byrum and Laurel Keith
Salem, OR

706. Two Score and Seven Stars
70" x 70", Thelma Childers and Judi Madsen
Charleston, IL

Nottingham Star pattern by Beth Fuller, Grace's Dowry Quilts

707. Jet Trails #11, 72" x 72"
Marcia DeCamp, Palmyra, NY

Pineapple Splash pattern from *Rich Traditions: Scrap Quilts to Paper Piece* by Nancy Mahoney, Martingale & Company, ©2002

708. Lighthouse Cottage by the Sea
71" x 71", Camelia Elliott, Pilot, VA

709. My Color Wheel Exploded
66" x 77", Dorinda Evans, Madison, MS

710. Asian Illusions, 63" x 54"
Cindy Garcia, Racine, WI

711. Appliqué Affair, 71" x 71"
Grayce G. Jahnke, Plymouth, MN

Appliqué Affair pattern by Edyta Sitar, Laundry Basket Quilts

Stars over Ft. Sumter pattern by Paula Barnes, Red Crinoline Quilts

Vintage Valentine by Verna Mosquera

712. Fiesta Stars, 67" x 67"
Allan Jones and Dot Collins,
San Antonio, TX

713. Vintage Valentine Variation
99" x 99", Jane Kahlig, Temple, TX

714. Water Earth and Spirit
66" x 66", Sue Krause, Princeville, IL

715. Spring Is in the Air, 62" x 62"
Terri Krysan, Lakeville, MN

716. Harmony Within, 71" x 81"
Sue McCarty, Roy, UT

Inspired by School House block

717. School Days, 68" x 68"
Margaret McDonald and Susan Campbell
Bendigo DC, Victoria, Australia

718. Civil War Ancestral Tribute
75" x 75", Sheri Mecom, Bedford, TX

The Civil War Diary Quilt by Rosemary Youngs, Krause Publications, ©2005; *The Civil War Love Letter Quilt* by Rosemary Youngs, Krause Publications, ©2007

719. Jewel Box, 66" x 66"
Cheri Meineke-Johnson and
Linda V. Taylor, Corinth, TX

Inspired by many, many antique quilts

720. Old Bear Tracks, 69" x 69"
Diane Pitchford, Gilbert, AZ

The Garden pattern by Jen Delyth ©2007 – www.celticartstudio.com

721. The Garden, 72" x 79"
Helia Ricci, Sunrise, FL

722. Bridezilla, 78" x 78"
Helen Roemisch, West Columbia, TX

Bali Wedding Star pattern by Judy and Bradley Niemeyer, Judy Niemeyer Quilting

723. Sputnik Stars, 63" x 63"
Joanne Adams Roth, Vancouver, WA

Inspired by the Endless Chain block

724. Catena, 67" x 62"
Timna Tarr, South Hadley, MA

725. Color Cubes, 75" x 60"
Eileen Vince, Livonia, MI

726. Moorish Memories, 77" x 77"
Cindy Williams, Olympia, WA

727. Avatar Revisited, 67" x 67"
Judy Woodworth, Gering, NE

Inspired by a Mystery Quilt Workshop by Mark Lipinski

Peek-a-Boo Lace designed by Jeanne Laurie. Pattern available in *Quiltmaker's Quilting and Embroidery*, Spring 2010 Digital issue, quiltmaker.com

728. Autumn Lace, 70" x 95"
Charlotte Wright and Linda Farrall
Stillwater, OK

729. Woods and Wildflowers
86" x 86", Jane Zillmer, Mercer, WI

801. Gogh Phish, 83" x 91"
Florence Stahl Calhoun, Corvallis, OR

802. Jack, 73" x 43"
Sandy Curran, Newport News, VA

803. Hot Africa, 99" x 48"
Janneke de Vries-Bodzinga
Kollumerzwaag, Friesland, The Netherlands

804. Laid Aside for Winter, 63" x 42"
Rebecca A. Douglas, Punta Gorda, FL

805. Sequoia Duck Pond, 77" x 87"
Pat Durbin, Eureka, CA

806. Coneflower Fiesta, 63" x 46"
Ann Fahl, Racine, WI

Inspired by a photograph taken by Gary Durbin

Figures inspired by British and American magazine illustrations and advertisements from 1895-1920

807. By the Sea, *76" x 66"*
Carol Goddu
Mississauga, Ontario, Canada

Inspired by a Designing from Nature workshop by Ruth McDowell

808. Through the Waters, *70" x 47"*
Suzanne Kistler, Visalia, CA

809. The Monumental Way
60" x 76", Karlyn Bue Lohrenz
Billings, MT

810. Cirque 2 Bird's Eye View
70" x 70", Meta MacLean
TMR Montreal, Quebec, Canada

Inspired by Cirque du Soleil

It's All About Triangles from *Freddy and Gwen Collaborate Again: Freewheeling Twists on Traditional Quilt Designs* by Gwen Marston and Freddy Moran, Lark Books, ©2009

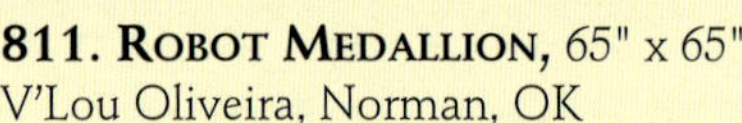

811. Robot Medallion, 65" x 65"
V'Lou Oliveira, Norman, OK

812. Proceed with Caution, 68" x 57"
Gayle Pulley, Eatonville, WA

813. Eagle! 65" x 69"
Linda Ross, Lake St. Louis, MO

814. Kazenobon, 80" x 81"
Masako Sakagami
Toyama, Toyama, Japan

815. Venetian Menagerie, 61" x 67"
Melissa Sobotka, Richardson, TX

816. Mulligana – The Goddess of Golf
85" x 87", Debra Svitil, Alpharetta, GA

817. Dawn Prayers on the Ganges
81" x 48", Meri Henriques Vahl
Soquel, CA

818. Witches Brew, 90" x 60"
Cathy Wiggins, Macon, NC

Magical Medallions pattern by Karen Kay Buckley, ©Karen Kay Buckley

901. Robyn's Flower Garden
81" x 81", Bobbette Brady
Uniontown, OH

902. Watermelon Time, 88" x 88"
Janet Brown, Gainesville, TX

903. Blended Baskets, 73" x 90"
Jean Cable, Mooresville, NC

904. Come September, 104" x 104"
Barbara Cascelli, Murrieta, CA

Patterns from *The Heart of Roses Quilt* by C. Jean Horst, ©Good Books, ©1994, <http://www.cjeanhorst.com>; A *Celtic Garden* by Philomena Durcan, Celtic Design Co., ©1995

Inspired by quilts in the American Folk Art Museum exhibition *Infinite Variety: Three Centuries of Red and White Quilts*, Park Avenue Armory, 2011

905. My Tribute to the Infinite Variety: Three Centuries of Red and White Quilts Show, 66" x 80", Thelma Childers, Charleston, IL

906. Branson Remix, 73" x 87"
Debby Cresanto, Millington, TN

907. Royal Amethyst, 72" x 72"
Rachelle Denneny, Glenelg North
South Australia, Australia

908. Radiant Star, 91" x 91"
Jennifer Emry, Arlington, VA

Inspired by an antique Radiant Star quilt from an exhibition of Quaker quilts at the Virginia Quilt Museum

909. Prometheus, 104" x 127"
Ferret, North Harrow, Middlesex
United Kingdom

910. Robyn's Renaissance on Point
86" x 87", Deborah France, San Antonio, TX

Robyn's Renaissance pattern by Jenny Haskins from *Creative Expressions* magazine, issues 23/24, ©2009; machine embroidery designs from Jenny Haskins Special Edition design CD *Robyn's Romance*, ©Jenny Haskins Designs

911. Kaleidoscope, 88" x 88"
Betty Gholson, Raleigh, IL

Inspired by a quilt in the American Folk Art Museum from the collection of Joanna S. Rose; and Paula Nadelstern's KALEIDOSCOPE quilt from *The Twentieth Century's Best American Quilts*, Mary Leman Austin, editor, Primedia, ©1999

912. Galhexy, 86" x 93"
Laney Henderson, Angels Camp, CA

Designs inspired by *One-Block Wonders: One Fabric, One Shape, One-of-a-Kind Quilts* by Maxine Rosenthal, C&T Publishing, ©2006; and spiral galaxy photos from the NASA website

Embroidery designs ©Embroidery Library Inc., emblibrary.com

913. Montana Sampler, 95" x 95"
Lorrie Hockett, Havre, MT

Inspired by an antique quilt from The Ultimate Quilting Book: Over 1,000 Inspirational Ideas and Practical Tips by Maggie McCormick Gordon, Collins & Brown, ©2000

914. Gig's Girls, 74" x 84"
Vicki Hodge, Westville, IN

915. The Battleground Quilt
101" x 116", Kathy Honeycutt
Columbus, MS

1776 quilt pattern from *The 1776 Quilt: Heartache, Heritage, and Happiness* by Pam Holland, Breckling Press, ©2007

916. Peggy's Poppies, 100" x 100"
Carol Hostetler, Battle Ground, WA

California poppies, bugs, and critters patterns from *Wildflowers: Designs for Appliqué & Quilting*, ©2010, and *Butterflies and Blooms*,©2002, by Carol Armstrong, C&T Publishing; SHALIMAR GARDEN by Lorraine Simmons from *The Visual Dance: Creating Spectacular Quilts* by Joen Wolfrom, C&T Publishing, ©2009; Poppies pattern from *Floral Appliqué: Original Designs and Techniques for Medallion Quilts* by Nancy Pearson, EZ Quilting by Wrights, ©1994

917. The Beginning, 87" x 92"
Manisha Hunt, Ormeau
Queensland, Australia

918. Loftily Poised in the Ether Capacious, 93" x 93", Rosalind Hunt
Lexington, SC

919. Pat's Promise, 72" x 82"
Patricia A. Isaman, Harrodsburg, KY

920. Peter Rabbit Hide and Seek
78" x 80', Seiko Kitagawa
Sapporo, Hokkaido, Japan

Junko Saito workshop; The World of Peter Rabbit pattern, ©Lecien Corporation, Japan

First AQS Entry – Large, 1st Entry in an AQS Paducah Contest

Block patterns from *More Conway Album Blocks: Baskets*,©1997, and *More Conway Album Blocks: Blue Birds*, ©2000, by Irma Gail Hatcher, Hatcher and Associates, Inc.

921. Birds and Baskets, 95" x 98"
Kate Klein, Lake Forest, IL

Crystal Treasures pattern designed by Liz Schwartz and Stephen Seifert. Pattern available from www.eQuiltPatterns.com.

922. Golden Anniversary, 85" x 85"
Cindy Ladig, South Charleston, OH

923. Blossoms of Love, 72" x 80"
Debbie Lambert, Indianapolis, IN

Birds & Blooms pattern by Jana Davidson, Turnberry Lane Patterns, ©2007

924. Illusion, 92" x 104"
Kathy Lyon and Allison Payette, Goshen, IN

Illusion pattern by Dereck C. Lockwood, ©Lockwood Enterprises

First AQS Entry – Large, 1st Entry in an AQS Paducah Contest

Muncy Compass pattern by D. Grick, B. Neff, and J. Youngman, Muncy Historical Society & Museum, Muncy, PA

925. The Compass Quilt, 98" x 98"
Kathleen McLaughlin, Noank, CT

Inspired by Whig Rose Variation by Elizabeth Gary Hudson, ca. 1850, from the collection of the Illinois State Museum, Springfield, Illinois

926. Whig Rose, 81" x 82"
Susan Ott, Bradenton, FL

927. French Braid, 104" x 110"
Cecelia Portlock, Barnhart, MO

Pattern from *French Braid Quilts: 14 Quick Quilts with Dramatic Results* by Jane Hardy Miller with Arlene Netten, C&T Publishing, ©2006

928. Not a "Plain Jane", 85" x 85"
Sue Schwegler, Plainfield, IL

Patterns from *Dear Jane: The Two Hundred Twenty-Five Patterns from the 1863 Jane A. Stickle Quilt* by Brenda Manges Papadakis, EZ Quilting by Wrights, ©1996

Fanfare for the Heroes pattern from *Scraps* by Judy Martin, ©Crosley-Griffith Publishing Company, Inc., ©2006

929. FANFARE FOR THE HEROES
94" x 94", Nancy Smith, Lake Forest, IL

Bethlehem Star workshop with Lois Miller, Cumberland County Piecemakers Quilt Guild

930. BETHLEHEM STAR, 85" x 85"
Marvell L. Stevens, Crossville, TN

931. SUMMER FAIRY, 65" x 83"
Kazue Tsukayama, Kaga, Ishikawa, Japan

932. SUNFLOWER STARS, 84" x 84"
Joy Voltenburg, Sullivan, IL

First AQS Entry – Large, *1st Entry in an AQS Paducah Contest*
First AQS Entry – Small, *1st Entry in an AQS Paducah Contest*

933. Unconventional Sue
100" x 100", Cindy Williams
Olympia, WA

934. Wrapped in Gentleness, 80" x 83"
Hiromi Yokota
Yokohama, Kanagawa, Japan

1001. Twisty Curvy Explosion
60" x 72", Kathie Beltz, Greenfield, NH

Design inspiration from Victorian Table Runner pattern #SWD411 by Annette Ornelas, ©Southwind Designs; and Monterrey Medallion pattern by Terry Atkinson, ©Atkinson Designs

1002. Eggplant Casserole, 56" x 68"
Anita Bowen, Columbia, SC

Vineyard Stars pattern by Judith Sandstrom from *Quilter's World* magazine, May issue, ©1998

First AQS Entry – Small, *1st Entry in an AQS Paducah Contest*

Jo's Whig Rose pattern from *Traditions* by Jo Morton for Jo Morton Quilts, Nebraska City, NE

1003. My Whig Rose, 57" x 57"
Caryl Brix, Wautoma, WI

1004. My Jungle Garden, 48" x 76"
Susan Cronenwett, Waldport, OR

1005. Waterwheels III, 40" x 40"
Cynthia Harrell Felts, Rolla, MO

Wheels of Whimsy pattern, designed by Wendy Hager, ©*Quilt Sampler* magazine, 1999

1006. Sun Salutation, 43" x 43"
Janice Head, Windsor, CA

Sedona Star pattern from a Precision Piecing workshop with Sally Collins, ©Sally Collins

First AQS Entry – Small, *1st Entry in an AQS Paducah Contest*

Liberated Log Cabins workshop with Gwen Marston

1007. Funky Log Cabin, 43" x 58"
Dorothy Heidemann-Nelson
Lincoln, NE

1008. St. Marks National Wildlife Refuge #1, 40" x 40"
Barbara Hoagland, Tallahassee, FL

1009. Last of the Blueberries
57" x 56", JoAnn Hoffman, Hill City, SD

1010. 2 Rue LaCroix, 46" x 57"
Susan Hoffmeier and Sandra Thompson
Iola, KS

1011. Backyard Beauties, 43" x 60"
Lori Kelley, New Philadelphia, OH

1012. If Leaves Could Choose, 48" x 56"
Priscilla Kibbee, Wolcott, NY

1013. Bloomin' Things, 48" x 48"
Carol Kolf, Sheridan, WY

1014. The ABC's of Recycling – The Cat's Meow, 42" x 54"
June M. Krause, Benton, KY

Flower Power workshop with Mary Lou Weidman

Cat Alphabet embroidery patterns, ©The Vermillion Stitchery, http://www.embroiderydesigns.com

First AQS Entry – Small, *1st Entry in an AQS Paducah Contest*

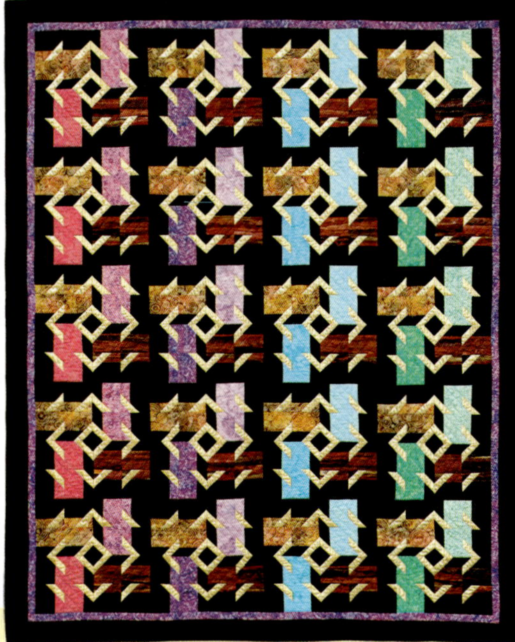

1015. Kaleidoscope Weave
60" x 75", Susan Lane, Vallejo, CA

Home & Harvest quilt pattern series by Erica Kaprow from *Quiltmaker* magazine, ©2005

1016. Home & Harvest, 51" x 53"
Sylvia L. Ledbetter, Fordyce, AR

1017. South of the Border
60" x 74", Judy Lowery, Franklin, NC

Woodsong pattern from *By Request: 10th Anniversary Edition* by Kathryn Squibb and Deborah Jacobs, ©Gathering Friends

1018. For Just One Day, 57" x 57"
Joanne MacNevin, Pembroke, MA

1019. CLOUDS IN MY LATTE, 56" x 74"
Karen Marchetti, Port St Lucie, FL

1020. EAST INDIES SPICE, 47" x 49"
Linda O'Donnell, Hoschton, GA

1021. THE THORN BIRDS, 60" x 60"
Kyungsu Park, Anyang-si, South Korea

1022. BLUE-VIOLET CIRCLE-SPHERE
42" x 42", Candice Phelan, Wellington, FL

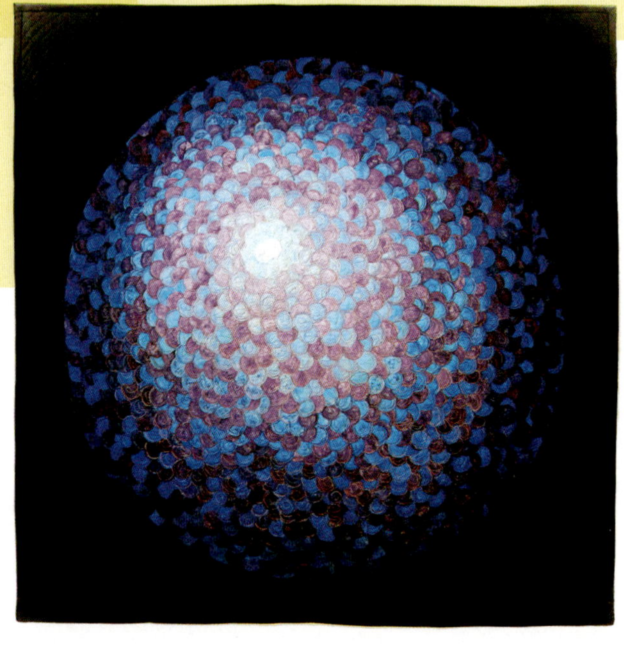

Raven and the Wind pattern by Ricky Tims from *Desert Visions – Rhapsody Quilts: Design Companion Vol. 2 to Ricky Tims' Rhapsody Quilts Bonus Appliqué, Designs & Ideas*, C&T Publishing, ©2009; Spirit pattern by Toni Whitney, ©Bigfork Bay Cotton Company

1023. Spirit Landing, 55" x 55"
Diane Phillips, Ennis, MT

Autumn Eyes pattern by Toni Whitney, ©Bigfork Bay Cotton Company

1024. Return Home, 49" x 73"
Beverley Raptis, White, GA

1025. Bonsai for Buddley, 55" x 58"
Joan Seidlitz and Dian Keepers
Napavine, WA

1026. First Baltimore, 59" x 59"
Gail H. Smith, Barrington, IL

13-block diagonal setting from *Mimi Dietrich's Baltimore Basics: Album Quilts from Start to Finish*, Martingale & Company, ©2006

First AQS Entry – Small, *1st Entry in an AQS Paducah Contest*

Appliqué quilt pattern from Hello! My Patchwork by Kathy Nakajima

1027. Rose Abundance, 58" x 58"
Sherry Southgate
Cambridge, Ontario, Canada

1028. B. S. I Love You, 58" x 68"
Janet Stone, Overland Park, KS

1029. Some Are My Own
41" x 51", Christa Strohmaier
Ried, Austria

1030. Yolk Music, 41" x 52"
Timna Tarr, South Hadley, MA

First AQS Entry – Small, 1st Entry in an AQS Paducah Contest

1031. Pineapple Trio, 48" x 48"
Margaret Teruya, Kaneohe, HI

Feathered Stars pattern from *Simple Traditions: 14 Quilts to Warm Your Home* by Kim Diehl, Martingale & Company, ©2006

1032. Turning Corners, 52" x 52"
Rod Turner, Johnston, IA

1033. Riot at the Gates, 57" x 66"
Molly Washburn, Bessemer, AL

1034. Let the Vines Shine Thru
49" x 49", Jackie White
Manitowaning, Ontario, Canada

First AQS Entry – Small, *1st Entry in an AQS Paducah Contest*
Small Wall Quilts, *Hand Quilted*

Based on the Spring panel from the Four Seasons window in the collection of the Charles Hosmer Morse Museum of American Art, Winter Park, Florida, with permission

Design inspired by an illustration by Ivan Bilibin in 1905 for Alexander Pushkin's *Tale of Tsar Saltan*

1035. Homage to Spring, 45" x 49"
Susan E. Ziel, Ocala, FL

1101. The Tsar's Decree, 52" x 41"
Megan Farkas, Sanbornton, NH

1102. Best Wishes!, 51" x 51"
Mikyung Jang, Seoul, South Korea

1103. Crème de la Crème, 52" x 77"
Bonnie Keller, Chehalis, WA

Korean Lucky Pattern by Dukyum-Kim, Hyunseul publisher

Inspired by the works of textile designer William Morris (1834-1896)

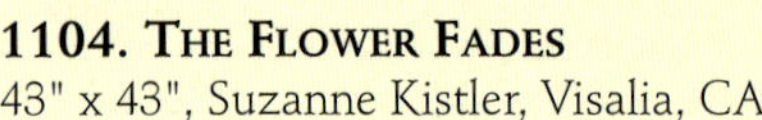

1104. The Flower Fades
43" x 43", Suzanne Kistler, Visalia, CA

1105. Memory, 40" x 40"
Ikuyo Kitada
Yokohama, Kanagawa, Japan

1106. Chatty Garden, 47" x 47"
Michiko Meike, Sapporo, Hokkaido, Japan

1107. Himawari - Flowers in Late Summer, 57" x 68", Hisako Naito
Tokushima, Tokushima, Japan

Junko Saito workshop; *Follow-the-Line Quilting Designs* ©Mary M. Covey Designs, marycoveydesigns.com

Kayoko Oguri Quilt Squares workshop

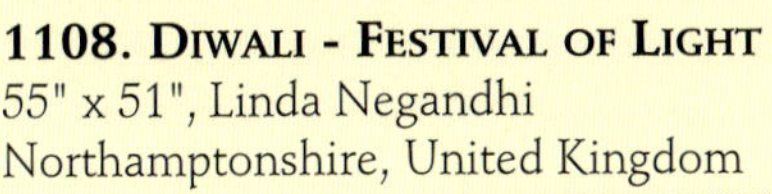

1108. Diwali - Festival of Light
55" x 51", Linda Negandhi
Northamptonshire, United Kingdom

1109. Jazzy Chicks, 46" x 47"
Hallie H. O'Kelley, Tuscaloosa, AL

1110. Four Gentlemen (Plum Blossom, Orchid, Chrysanthemum, and Bamboo)
60" x 60", Young Sil Park, Incheon, South Korea

1111. Land of Liberty, 57" x 70"
Pat Wagner, Gooding, ID

Patterns by Dinah Jeffries, ©Garden City Gateworks

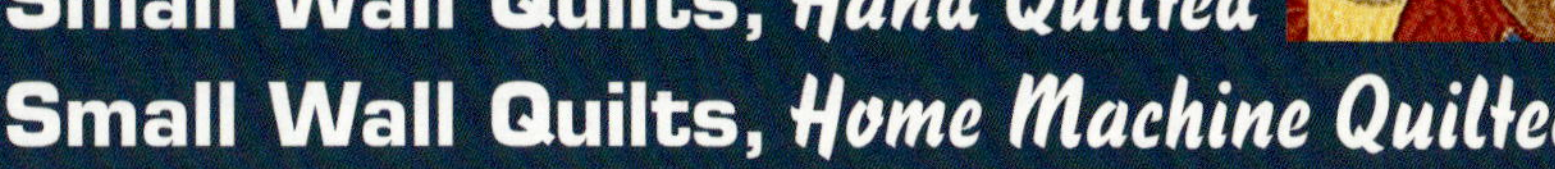

Junko Saito workshop

1112. Dear My Dogs, 47" x 47"
Akemi Yasuda, Ishikari, Hokkaido, Japan

1201. Woodland Treasure, 40" x 40"
Frieda Anderson, Elgin, IL

1202. Tessellating Wings, 53" x 64"
Wendy Butler Berns, Lake Mills, WI

1203. Birds and Flowers, 41" x 42"
Beth Brady, Marietta, GA

1204. Favorite Things, 45" x 41"
Peggy Brown, Nashville, IN

Design inspiration from a floor section of the Historic Guenther House of Pioneer Flour Mills, San Antonio, Texas, used with permission

1205. Guenther House Tile, 58" x 58"
Carol W. Carpenter, Tucson, AZ

1206. Appian Way, 48" x 48"
Marcia DeCamp, Palmyra, NY

1207. Three Friends, 52" x 47"
Sheril Drummond, Lexington, KY

Inspired by a photo taken by Gary Durbin

1208. Baby Tigress, Sheena
51" x 41", Pat Durbin, Eureka, CA

1209. Seeking Balance, 44" x 44"
Karen Eckmeier, Kent, CT

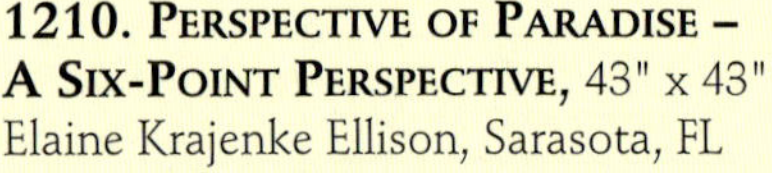

1210. Perspective of Paradise – A Six-Point Perspective, 43" x 43"
Elaine Krajenke Ellison, Sarasota, FL

1211. Aloe Vera, 48" x 78"
Grace J. Errea, Laguna Niguel, CA

1212. A View from Above, 40" x 63"
Sheila Frampton-Cooper, Van Nuys, CA

Quilted Village pattern by Janet Miller, ©The City Stitcher; border quilting designs inspired by Leah Day's Free-Motion Quilting blog

1213. Hartwell Commons, 54" x 58"
Sandra Gilreath, Macon, GA

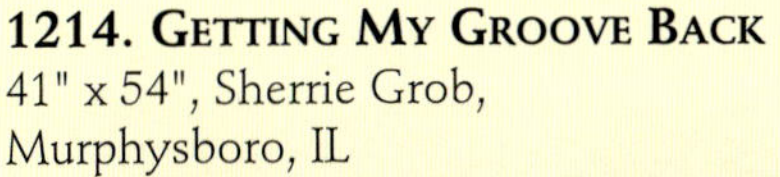

1214. Getting My Groove Back
41" x 54", Sherrie Grob,
Murphysboro, IL

1215. The Greens of Spring, 48" x 61"
Robin M. Haller, Carbondale, IL

1216. It's Time, 57" x 47"
Gloria Hansen, East Windsor, NJ

1217. Organic Matter, 45" x 47"
Barbara Oliver Hartman
Flower Mound, TX

1218. Imagining India, 49" x 56"
Pat Holly, Ann Arbor, MI

1219. Celtic 9-Patches, 42" x 42"
Jaynette Huff, Conway, AR

Celtic stencils from Mary Butler Shannon's *Everything Celtic*

Embroidered hearts from the Hearts Collection, ©Sarah Vedeler Designs

1220. Coeurs de la Soie, 51" x 51"
Patricia Kerko and Barbara Goodman
Sunset, SC

1221. Mexican Sunflowers, 41" x 55"
Karen Linduska, Carbondale, IL

AQS

1222. Numida I, 49" x 41"
Penelope Little, Salem, SC

1223. The Hues of Amber, 46" x 58"
Karlyn Bue Lohrenz, Billings, MT

Patterns from *Quilts from Aunt Amy* by Mary Tendall Etherington and Connie Tesene, Martingale and Company, ©1999

1224. Dishonor My Mother
54" x 53", Rebecca Muir MacKellar
Canton, NY

1225. If on a Winter's Eve, 40" x 51"
Janice Maddox, Asheville, NC

1226. Synergy, 54" x 53"
Nancy Sterett Martin, Owensboro, KY

1227. Dandy Lions, 44" x 44"
Barbara Barrick McKie, Lyme, CT

1228. Audubon's Christmas
47" x 52", Kathy McNeil, Tulalip, WA

Pattern from Ricky Tims' *Convergence Quilts: Mysterious, Magical, Easy, and Fun* by Ricky Tims, C&T Publishing, ©2003

1229. Fantasy, 59" x 66"
Mariko Miwa, Musashino, Tokyo, Japan

1230. Radiance, 59" x 59"
Sharon Murphy and
Georgianne Kandler, Seattle, WA

1231. Myopia, 49" x 49"
Judith Putnam, Paris, TN

1232. Fire Dance, 44" x 54"
Diana Shore, Bell Canyon, CA

1233. Two Bottles to Fill One Chalice, 53" x 44", Jen Siegrist
Milford, OH

1234. Floral Fantasy, 59" x 70"
Karen Hull Sienk, Colden, NY

1235. Fighting Dragons, 50" x 56"
Jan Soules, Elk Grove, CA

Credit: Assorted appliqué blocks from *Japanese Quilt Blocks to Mix & Match* by Susan Briscoe, Kodansha USA, ©2007

1236. Motherhood, 43" x 58"
Anna VanDemark, Butternut, WI

1237. My Brown Monkey, 52" x 70"
Mary T. Wakeley, Ottawa, IL

Monkey Business pattern designed by Evelyn Young, Marula Imports, ©2012

1238. Southern Delight
54" x 71", Mariya Waters
Melbourne, Victoria, Australia

1239. U-taupe-ia, 58" x 71"
Becky Weiland, King of Prussia, PA

1240. Zestful Zinnias, 52" x 50"
Sandra C. Werlich, Carbondale, IL

Surprisingly Red pattern ©Jacqueline de Jonge, BeColourful.com

1301. Butterflies for July Not Christmas, 60" x 60", Sandie Dolbee
Kalamazoo, MI

1302. The Gingko Tree, 50" x 48"
Barbara (Bobbe) Green and
Irene Reising, Paducah, KY

The Gingko pattern by Cheryl Wittmayer, ©Sew-Be-It.biz

1303. Peppermint Twist, 40" x 40"
Pam Hill, Brisbane, Queensland, Australia

Designs inspired by *600 Decorative Floral Designs* by F. B. Heald, Dover Publications, ©2008

Heartland pattern by Pearl P. Pereira, ©P3 Designs

1304. Heart Land, 59" x 64"
Lorrie Hockett, Havre, MT

1305. Midnight Blossoms, 44" x 47"
JoAnn Hoffman, Hill City, SD

1306. The Brooch, 57" x 57"
Richard Larson, Plano, TX

1307. Fiesta de los Angeles, 46" x 72"
Salli McQuaid, Walla Walla, WA

1308. Little Girl and Dog
59" x 62", Hiroko Miyama,
Chofu, Tokyo, Japan

Batik Wheels workshop and pattern, ©Deb Karasik

1309. Paper Moon, 42" x 42"
Helen Roemisch, West Columbia, TX

1310. Bounty, 48" x 72"
Mark L. Sherman, Coral Springs, FL

Inspired by the *Lady with Fruit* lithograph by Alfonse Maria Mucha, 1897

1311. Blooming Baskets, 40" x 59"
Gail H. Smith, Barrington, IL

Blooming Baskets pattern from *Friendship Strips & Scraps* by Edyta Sitar, Landauer Publishing, LLC, ©2010, www.landauercorp.com

Appliqué design inspiration from Simple Pleasures pattern "Auntie's Garden," ©Cynthia Tomaszewski

1312. HAPPINESS IS, 57" x 71"
Bonnie Stetson, Pinehurst, NC

Block patterns from *My Whimsical Quilt Garden: 20 Bird and Flower Blocks to Appliqué* from Piece 'O Cake Designs by Becky Goldsmith and Linda Jenkins, C&T Publishing, ©2010

1313. WHIMSY...TO THE MAX
58" x 58", Joyce Stewart,
Deweyville, UT

1314. AUTUMN KEPT, 45" x 55"
Deanna Tachick, Suring, WI

1315. INSPIRATION GARDEN
46" x 58", Alice Tignor
Severna Park, MD

The Calico Garden Quilt pattern by Froncie Quinn, ©Hoopla Patterns Shelburne Museum Collection, from the 1950 quilt by Florence Cowdin Peto. Quilt owned by Shelburne Museum, Shelburne, Vermont.

1316. Two Dozen Roses, 53" x 53"
Monica Troy, Lemont, IL

1317. I Love the Nightlife
57" x 57", Jane Zillmer, Mercer, WI

1401. Remembrance, 49" x 53"
Rosalie Baker, Davenport, IA

1402. The Wrath of Poseidon,
59" x 53", Marilyn Belford,
Chenango Forks, NY

1403. Georgia on My Mind, 48" x 45"
Nancy S. Brown, Oakland, CA

1404. You Can Never Have Too Many Tulips, 49" x 40"
Peggy Brown, Nashville, IN

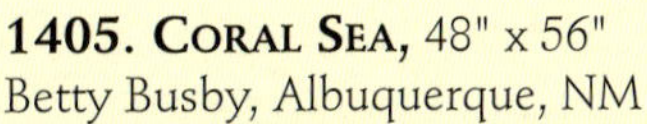

1405. Coral Sea, 48" x 56"
Betty Busby, Albuquerque, NM

1406. Peaceful Pond, 48" x 60"
Carol Daniels and Steve Daniels
Sapphire, NC

1407. Nature's Backyard, 42" x 52"
Vicki David, Santa Rosa, CA

1408. Fire Flower, 45" x 40"
Pat Durbin, Eureka, CA

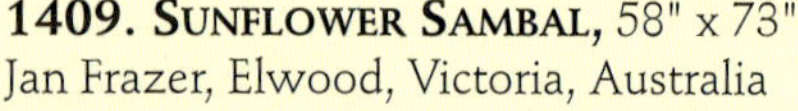

1409. Sunflower Sambal, 58" x 73"
Jan Frazer, Elwood, Victoria, Australia

1410. Faith Alone, 46" x 62"
Jerry Granata, Ft. Pierce, FL

Design inspired by a photograph by Rein Nomm www.nomm.com

1411. Out in the Garden, 49" x 48"
Leslie A. Hall, Longboat Key, FL

1412. Grandma's Plate, 43" x 43"
Linda M. Haltom, Crawfordsville, IN

1413. The Hen Party, 46" x 46"
Beth Porter Johnson, Houston, TX

1414. Montana Tigers, 50" x 61"
Karlyn Bue Lohrenz, Billings, MT

1415. Fairer Still the Moonlight
55" x 53", Rebecca Muir MacKellar
Canton, NY

1416. Oh No, Scuba Cat
54" x 42", Nancy Sterett Martin
Owensboro, KY

1417. Queen Nemo, 53" x 44"
Bridget Wilson Matlock, Alcoa, TN

1418. Climbing Beauty, 54" x 42"
Barbara Barrick McKie, Lyme, CT

1419. Jellie Snacks, 42" x 52"
Kathy McNeil, Tulalip, WA

1420. Sakura Sakura, 52" x 62"
Hiroko Miyama, Chofu, Tokyo, Japan

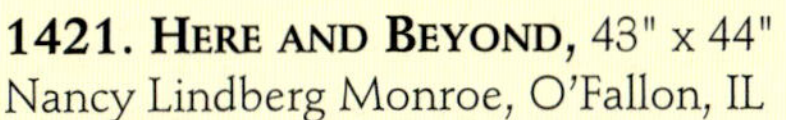

1421. Here and Beyond, 43" x 44"
Nancy Lindberg Monroe, O'Fallon, IL

1422. A Welcome Oasis
48" x 66", Thelma Moyer
Belfair, WA

Venetian Tiles pattern from *Stack-n-Whackier Quilts* by Bethany S. Reynolds, American Quilter's Society, ©2001

1423. Poster Beau, 52" x 43"
Betty New, Naples, FL

1424. Mount Moran, 42" x 61"
Charles O'Kelley, Tuscaloosa, AL

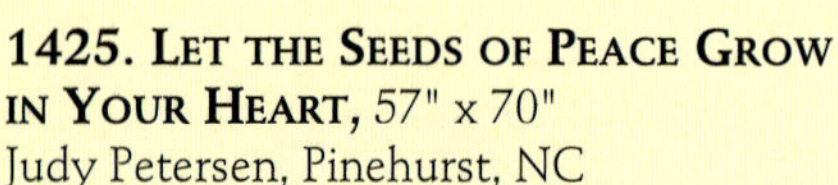

1425. Let the Seeds of Peace Grow in Your Heart, 57" x 70"
Judy Petersen, Pinehurst, NC

Inspired by an original design by Deb Dittmer

1426. Foxglove Fairy, 42" x 41"
Ruth Powers, Carbondale, KS

1427. Lela Duchess of Pahrump
53" x 58", Cheri Rabourn and
Nancy Lobsinger, Lee's Summit, MO

1428. Native Americans
48" x 42", Jen Siegrist, Milford, OH

1429. Hollyhocks, 42" x 53"
Karen Hull Sienk, Colden, NY

1430. A Fragile Garden in the Sea, 48" x 43"
Shirley Stevenson, Sherman, TX

Homecoming Wreath pattern from *Little Quilts: All Through the House* by Alice Berg, Sylvia Johnson, and Mary Ellen Von Holt, Martingale & Co, ©1993; President's Wreath pattern from *Miniature Quilts* magazine #51, ©2001

1501. My Way, 14" x 14"
Elaine Braun, Paducah, KY

1502. President's Wreath, 8" x 8"
Annette M. Burgess, Union City, PA

1503. New York Minute, 21" x 21"
Kathleen L. Carlson, Bridgeton, MO

1504. Tea Leaves, 18" x 20"
Linda Dyken, Mobile, AL

New York Minute pattern from *Fons & Porter's Love of Quilting* magazine, July/August issue, ©2005

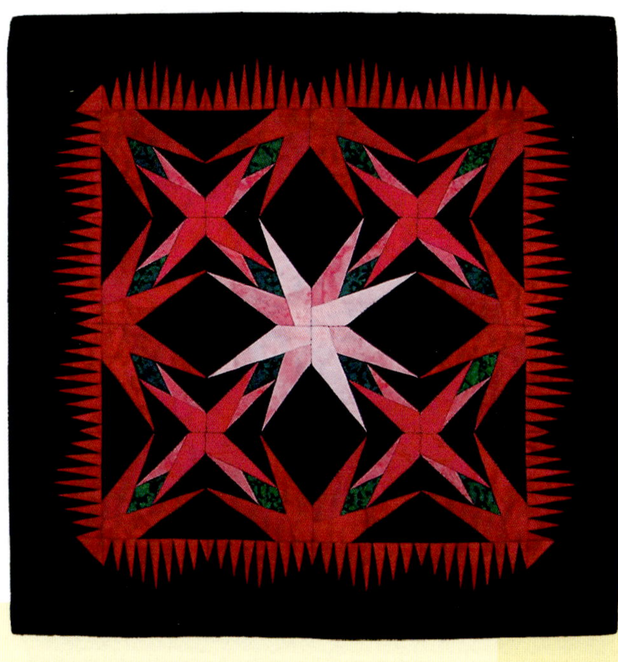

Cindi's Block from *40 Bright & Bold Paper-Pieced Blocks: 12-Inch Designs* by Carol Doak, Martingale and Company, ©2002

1505. Inner Glow, 11" x 11"
Janet Frank, Tallahassee, FL

1506. Monochromatic, 14" x 14"
Kumiko Frydl, Houston, TX

1507. Golden Snowflake, 22" x 22"
Renae Haddadin, Sandy, UT

1508. Springtime, 14" x 14"
Jane Holihan, Walworth, NY

Tooled Leather digitized pattern, ©JoAnn Hoffman; Christmas Collection digitized embroidery, ©OESD, embroideryonline.com

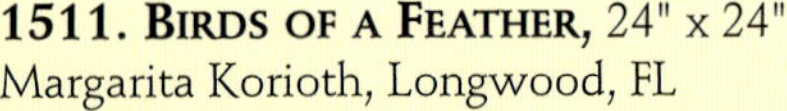

1509. Dixie Doodles, 21" x 21"
Judy Ingram, Paducah, KY

1510. One Plus Twelve, 18" x 18"
Margit Kagerer, Carefree, AZ

1511. Birds of a Feather, 24" x 24"
Margarita Korioth, Longwood, FL

1512. Strawberry Starburst
13" x 13", Vicki Littel,
Menomonee Falls, WI

Venetian Tiles pattern from *Stack-n-Whackier Quilts* by Bethany S. Reynolds, American Quilter's Society, ©2001

Blooming Tale pattern ©Jacqueline de Jonge, BeColourful.com

1513. I Got Lost, 17" x 18"
Masanobu Miyama, Chofu, Tokyo, Japan

1514. Springtime, 9" x 11"
Mary-Margaret Morton
Ann Arbor, MI

1515. Little Sugar Star, 13" x 15"
Lorraine Olsen, Springfield, MO

1516. Flowers from Grandmother's Secret Garden, 24" x 20"
Diana Perry, Hot Springs, AR

1517. America the Beautiful II
16" x 13", Sharon L. Schlotzhauer
Colorado Springs, CO

1518. Betwixt & Between, 8" x 11"
George Siciliano, Lebanon, PA

1519. From the Schooner Coast
21" x 21", Sarah Ann Smith, Hope, ME

1520. Dainty and Delightful
10" x 11", Mildred Sorrells
Macomb, IL

Inspired by an antique Variable Star quilt, ca. 1890

1521. Cheddar Stars Over Moab
19" x 24", Sandra Starley, Moab, UT

Design inspired by a trip to the Lancaster Quilt & Textile Museum, Lancaster, PA; and fabrics at the Old Country Store, Intercourse, PA

1522. Amish Center Diamond
20" x 20", Virginia Stentz, St. Louis, MO

1523. Mini Magic, 20" x 20"
Mariya Waters
Melbourne, Victoria, Australia

1524. Mo'orea Motifs, 19" x 19"
Diane Whittier, Shawnee, KS

Inspired by the antique FLORAL URNS quilt from *The Quilt Digest 2*, edited by Roderick Kiracofe and Michael Kile, ©1984

1525. Lilliputian Floral Urns
22" x 22", Mary Abbott Williams
Pinehurst, NC

Thank you, contestants, for sharing your quilts!

Index of Quilts

U

V

W

Y

Z

Suggestions for Good Photography

Picture this: You've spent months cutting, sewing, and striving for perfection. You've been up to your ears in batting, thread, and fabric. You've made the quilt of your dreams. After all that hard work, your quilt is finished. Your quilt entry has to get in the mail today! Frantically, you throw your quilt over a banister, shoot a picture, and get your entry in the mail. You may have just made the best quilt of your entire life. It may, in fact, be "Best of Show" worthy. But you're forgetting one important detail: In order for your quilt to hang in one of our shows, it must first be juried. How do we jury your quilts? You guessed it...by YOUR photography.

We've received our share of excellent photography...but we've also seen some of the worst. Below you will find some helpful hints to go by when photographing your next masterpiece! Remember, your pictures are all our juries can see...show your best work!

- **First, make sure your camera is on the highest quality setting.** This will, indeed, make your file sizes larger. This is NOT a problem. In most cases, the larger the file size, the better quality the image; the more megapixels you use, the better your photograph will be. Also, (and we can't stress this enough) be sure your camera is in focus when shooting your quilt.

- **The full shot image must be exactly what it says: a FULL shot.** This means no folded corners, no bushes or trees in front of the quilt, and no fingers peeking over the top. For the best results, suspend your quilt from a curtain rod, letting it hang freely. Shoot your quilt at a 90-degree angle from the CENTER of the quilt. If you shoot your quilt from above or below, the quilt does not appear square (see illustrations). Please do not crop your photos.

- **Use your best source of lighting.** The best results come when shooting outdoors on a cloudy day. The distilled sunlight creates just the right lighting for your quilts. Avoid harsh, direct sunlight as it blows out the color of your work. If you must shoot your quilt indoors, choose a room with the most natural lighting, and try to avoid any shadowing over your quilt.

- **When selecting your detail shot, choose a 12" section of your quilt that is your favorite.** You know your best work, so show it in your detail shot. Make sure you're not physically too close to your quilt when taking the picture, as your camera may have trouble focusing.

- **When finished, save your image as the highest quality JPEG and burn your image to a CD.** If you don't have the capability to save your image to a CD, simply take your camera or memory card to the nearest photo-processing center and they will be happy to do it for you. Do not crop or manipulate your photos.

Not only will your photographs be viewed by our jury, but if your quilt is selected to hang in any of our shows, your photograph will be published in our Catalogue of Show Quilts, digital or printed. We know you've worked hard on your quilt. Don't jeopardize your quilt's future with bad photography!

Timetable and Important Dates

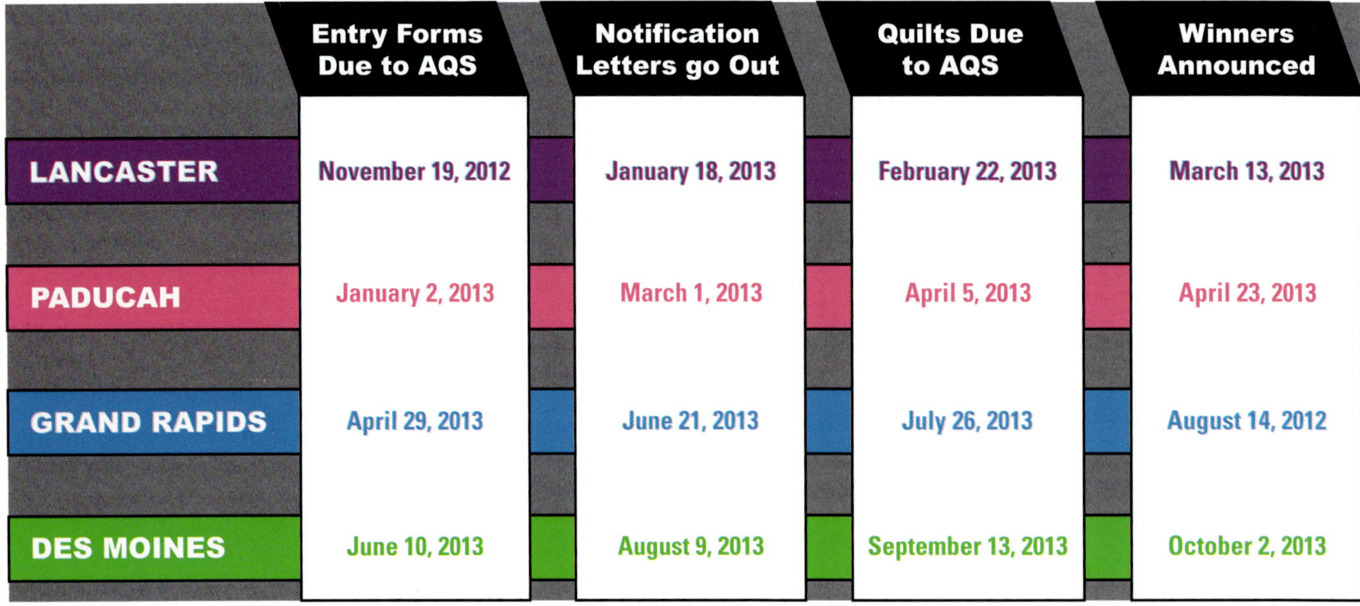

	Entry Forms Due to AQS	Notification Letters go Out	Quilts Due to AQS	Winners Announced
LANCASTER	November 19, 2012	January 18, 2013	February 22, 2013	March 13, 2013
PADUCAH	January 2, 2013	March 1, 2013	April 5, 2013	April 23, 2013
GRAND RAPIDS	April 29, 2013	June 21, 2013	July 26, 2013	August 14, 2012
DES MOINES	June 10, 2013	August 9, 2013	September 13, 2013	October 2, 2013

General Quilt Contest Rules

These Rules apply to all four 2013 AQS Quilt Contests

1. The maker(s) of a cloth quilt can enter their completed work by submitting the completed and signed entry form, entry fee of $10 per quilt for AQS members or $30 per quilt for non-members, and CD of digital images (see rule 5).

2. There is a limit of three entries per contestant, one entry per category. The name(s) on the top line of the entry form should be that of the maker/contestant(s). Those listed as "other stitchers on this quilt" will not be considered contestants and may have their own three entries.

3. All quilts must be quilted by hand, machine, or both. Quilting is defined as a running stitch that passes through top, batting, and backing. Tied quilts are not eligible.

4. All quilts must fit the size requirements and definitions of the selected category. Please see each entry form for category definitions and sizes. You must select one category for each quilt.
For categories defined by quilting method:

- **a.** Home Sewing Machine includes use of any sewing machine that is table-mounted/stationary, allowing the quilter to move the fabric rather than the machine.
- **b.** Longarm/Midarm Machine includes any sewing machine mounted on a frame, allowing the quilter to move the machine head rather than the fabric.

5. The 3 photos that must be submitted with the entry are:

1. A full-view digital photo of the quilt **must show all sides, edges, corners, and binding of the quilt.** No part of the quilt can be obscured. **Do not crop or manipulate your photos.**
2. A detail photo must show quilting stitches.
3. Please include a photo of the entrant(s), from the shoulders up.

Send only these three photos on your CD. Do not send slides or printed photos. CDs will not be returned. See page 15 for photography tips.

6. Quilts must be in excellent condition. Incomplete, torn, or soiled quilts do not qualify for entry or display.

7. Quilts winning cash awards in any previous AQS contest (Lancaster, Paducah, Knoxville, Grand Rapids, or Des Moines), or made from stamped kits are not eligible.

8. Quilts must be a single unit and may not be framed with wood, metal, etc.

9. All decisions of the jurors and judges are final. AQS reserves the right to reject any entry or to move a quilt into a different category. AQS juries quilts based on technique as well as appropriate subject matter.

The contest rules for all contests can be printed at: www.AmericanQuilter.com

Quilt detail: YOLK MUSIC by Timna Tarr, South Hadley, MA
Photographed by Stephen Petegorsky

Prize Money • $44,250 at all 3 shows:
Lancaster, Grand Rapids, and Des Moines

Best of Show $10,000
Best Hand Workmanship $5,000
Best Machine Workmanship $5,000
Best Longarm Workmanship $5,000
Best Wall Quilt $3,000

In All Categories:

1st Place $1,500
2nd Place $1,000
3rd Place $750

Paducah Prize Money $120,000

Janome Best of Show. $20,000*
AQS Hand Workmanship $12,000*
BERNINA Machine Workmanship $12,000*
APQS Longarm Machine Quilting $12,000*
Moda Best Wall $5,000*
Coats & Clark Wall Hand Workmanship . $3,000
Brother Wall Machine Workmanship $3,000
Handi Quilter Wall Longarm Machine Quilting $3,000
Benartex Best Miniature $3,000*

Categories 1–14:

1st Place $1,500
2nd Place $1,000
3rd Place $750

Category 15:

1st Place $500
2nd Place $300
3rd Place $200

*Purchase awards – These quilts become the property of The National Quilt Museum

American Quilter's Society
P. O. Box 3290 • Paducah, KY 42002-3290

Categories:

Lancaster

A. Bed Quilts – Hand Quilted
B. Bed Quilts – Machine Quilted
C. Wall Quilts – Hand Quilted
D. Wall Quilts – Home Machine Quilted
E. Wall Quilts – Longarm/Midarm Machine Quilted

Paducah

1. Bed Quilts – Hand Quilted
2. Bed Quilts – Home Machine Quilted
3. Bed Quilts – Longarm/Midarm Machine Quilted
4. 1st AQS Paducah Entry – Large
5. Large Wall Quilts – Hand Quilted
6. Large Wall Quilts – Home Machine Quilted
7. Large Wall Quilts – Longarm/Midarm Machine Quilted
8. Large Wall Quilts – Pictorial
9. Group Quilts
10. Small Wall Quilts – Hand Quilted
11. Small Wall Quilts – Home Machine Quilted
12. Small Wall Quilts – Longarm/Midarm Machine Quilted
13. Small Wall Quilts – Pictorial
14. 1st AQS Paducah Entry – Small
15. Miniature Quilts

Grand Rapids

A. Quilter's Choice
B. Made by Machine
C. Wall Quilts – Hand Quilted
D. Wall Quilts – Machine Quilted
E. The Ultimate Guild Challenge

Des Moines

A. Bed Quilts – Hand Quilted
B. Bed Quilts – Machine Quilted
C. Wall Quilts – Hand Quilted
D. Wall Quilts – Machine Quilted
E. Fabric Art

2013 AQS QUILT SHOWS & CONTESTS

AQS brings you FOUR great quilt shows in 2013

Each venue features unique quilt contests with cash awards, workshops, and lectures—

and the world's finest Merchant Mall for quilters, with the very latest in quiltmaking products and tools.

Scan our logo to visit us on your Smartphone

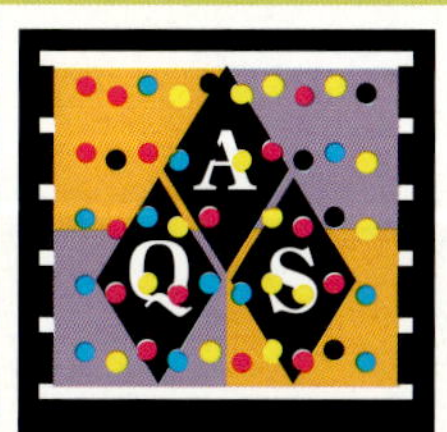

Get the free mobile app for your phone

http://gettag.mobi

For more info visit:

www.AmericanQuilter.com

270-898-7903

MARCH 13–16

4th ANNUAL

LANCASTER, PA

Lancaster County Convention Center

Many people are drawn to Lancaster County for its Amish community but soon discover and enjoy all the other things to see and do when they visit Pennsylvania Dutch Country, including the AQS Quilt Show & Contest!

APRIL 24–27

29th ANNUAL

PADUCAH, KY

Paducah Expo Center

The April AQS Quilt Show & Contest experience is legendary. The quilts are among the best in the world; the merchants have the latest books and supplies; and the teachers are the finest. Treat yourself to an extraordinary experience!

AUGUST 14–17

2nd ANNUAL

GRAND RAPIDS, MI

DeVos Place Convention Center

Big-city excitement and natural splendor. Cultural sophistication and small-town warmth. Grand Rapids offers the best of all worlds. Nearby hotels and abundant parking; it's all here, including the newest major quilt show in America!

OCTOBER 2–5

5th ANNUAL

DES MOINES, IA

Iowa Events Center

If Des Moines isn't your hometown, it will feel like it. Visit this four-time "All American City" to experience the cordial people, welcoming atmosphere, and outstanding quality of life in this capital city.

April 24–27, 2013

The following rules are specific to Paducah, Kentucky. To enter the Paducah quilt contest, please fill out the entry form on page 111. Good Luck!

Quilt Entry Deadline: January 2, 2013

Rules Specific for Paducah, Kentucky 2013

P1. All General Quilt Contest Rules on Page 2 apply.
P2. Quilts must have been finished between January 1, 2011 and the entry deadline.
P3. Quilts must be available for display from April 6, 2013 until one week after the show.
P4. Quilts must fit within the size requirements and definitions of the categories below.
P5. Quilts in all categories except Category 9 must have been made by no more than 2 people.

Bed Quilts: Width 60" to 110"; Length 80" or more. Quilts designed for use on a bed.

1. **Bed Quilts – Hand Quilted:** quilted predominantly by hand.
2. **Bed Quilts – Home Machine Quilted:** quilted predominantly by home sewing machine.
3. **Bed Quilts – Longarm/Midarm Machine Quilted:** quilted predominantly by longarm/midarm machine.
4. **1st Entry in an AQS Paducah Contest – Large:** contestant(s) must not have been semifinalist(s) in any previous AQS Paducah quilt contest.

Large Wall Quilts: Width 60" to 110"; Length 40" or more.
Quilts designed for display on a wall.

5. **Large Wall Quilts – Hand Quilted:** quilted predominantly by hand.
6. **Large Wall Quilts – Home Machine Quilted:** quilted predominantly by home sewing machine.
7. **Large Wall Quilts – Longarm/Midarm Machine Quilted:** quilted predominantly by longarm/midarm machine.
8. **Large Wall Quilts – Pictorial:** representation of a person, place, or thing.

Group Quilt: Width 60" to 110"; Length 40" or more.

9. **Group:** made by 3 or more people.

Small Wall Quilts: Width 30" to 60"; Length 30" or more.
Quilts designed for display on a wall.

10. **Small Wall Quilts – Hand Quilted:** quilted predominantly by hand.
11. **Small Wall Quilts – Home Machine Quilted:** quilted predominantly by home sewing machine.
12. **Small Wall Quilts – Longarm/Midarm Quilted:** quilted predominantly by longarm/midarm machine.
13. **Small Wall Quilts – Pictorial:** representation of a person, place, or thing.
14. **1st Entry in an AQS Paducah Contest – Small:** contestant(s) must not have been semifinalist(s) in any previous AQS Paducah quilt contest.

Miniature Quilts: Width no more than 24"; Length no more than 24".

15. **Miniature:** all aspects of the quilt are reduced in scale.

Written judging evaluations are provided for each quilt exhibited in this contest.

OFFICE USE ONLY
QUILT # ________
STATUS ________
ENTRY # ________

AQS Quilt Show & Contest 2013 PADUCAH

Send in this entry form with CD-ROM, *Appraisal, and *Design Permissions (*if applicable). This form may be photocopied.

☐ Member **$10.00**
Membership Number ____________

☐ Non-Member **$30.00**

(Want to be a member? Check a box below.)

☐ 1 Year US Membership **$25.00**

☐ 1 Year International Membership **$45.00**

Entrant(s) or Group Name ____

(Please Print) (ONLY THESE Name(s) will be used in the Show Book)

Street ____

City ____________________ State ______ Country __________ Zip or Postal Code ____________

Phone ____________________ Cell ____________________ E-mail ____________________

Contact the city desk or feature editor at your newspaper to get an e-mail address; newspapers are requesting e-mailed press releases.

Complete Name of Newspaper ____________________ Newspaper E-mail ____________________

Select Your Category Number (see rule P5 on page 4 for more information):

Bed Quilts:
W 60" to 110"; L 80" or more
☐ 1. Hand Quilted
☐ 2. Home Machine
☐ 3. Longarm/Midarm Machine
☐ 4. 1st Entry – Paducah Contest – Large

Large Wall Quilts:
W 60" to 110"; L 40" or more
☐ 5. Hand Quilted
☐ 6. Home Machine
☐ 7. Longarm/Midarm Machine
☐ 8. Pictorial

Group Quilts:
W 60" to 110"; L 40" or more
☐ 9. Group

Small Wall Quilts:
W 30" to 60"; L 30" or more
☐ 10. Hand Quilted
☐ 11. Home Machine
☐ 12. Longarm/Midarm Machine
☐ 13. Pictorial
☐ 14. 1st Entry – Paducah Contest – Small

Miniature Quilts:
24" maximum, W and L
☐ 15. Miniature

Information About Your Entry:

Title ______________________________ Size in inches ________" width by ________" length

Approx. Insurance Value $ ________ (Over $1,000 requires a written appraisal **included with this form**. Maximum value is $5,000.)

Quilted by: ____________________ Other Stitchers: ____________________

____

Brief Description of Quilt for Show Book (25 words): ______________________________

____

Techniques: (Choose all that apply) ☐ Appliqué ☐ Piecing ☐ Embroidery ☐ Trapunto ☐ Needlework Technique ____________ ☐ Other ____________

Quilting: (Choose all that apply) (see general rule 4 on page 2) ☐ **Hand** ☐ **Home Sewing Machine** ☐ With Stitch Regulator ☐ **Longarm/Midarm Machine** ☐ With Stitch Regulator ☐ Computer-Assisted Stitch Software ☐ **Embroidery Machine**

Design Pattern Source: (Choose all that apply: Use separate paper for additional space.)

☐ Totally Original (Definition: first, not a copy of a previous work; new creation; patterns by others are NOT used.)
☐ Pattern(s) used; list pattern source (if any patterns were used, please list them below).
☐ Design inspired by another source (please list source of inspiration below).

Magazine ____________ Issue ________ Year ________ Project Title ____________

Pattern/Book title – List complete title ____________ Author ________ Publisher ________ Project Title ____________

Other Artwork title/type ____________ Contact Information for artist, publisher, or source ____________

Workshop Title ____________ Workshop Instructor ____________

Authorized by my signature below, I wish to enter the above item and agree to abide by all quilt contest rules as well as any decision of the jury and/or judges. I certify that this form has been filled out in its entirety and is complete, true and accurate to the best of my information, knowledge and belief. If my quilt becomes accepted in the American Quilter's Society (AQS) Show, I acknowledge and understand that my signature below gives AQS the right to use a photo of my quilt for promotion of the AQS Event for which it was entered in any publications, advertisements, Catalogue of Show Quilts, non-printable CD-Rom of show images, and other printed or electronic materials. I further understand that AQS will request permission before using the quilt entered for any other commercial purpose.

Please put your name on the CD-ROM and mail digital images (as outlined in the rules), completed entry blank, and fee for each quilt to:

American Quilter's Society,
Dept. Paducah 2013 Entry,
PO Box 3290, Paducah, KY 42002-3290
BY JANUARY 2, 2013

____
Signature

Credit Card (Visa, MasterCard, or Discover) Card Number ☐☐☐☐-☐☐☐☐-☐☐☐☐-☐☐☐☐ Exp. Date ☐☐☐☐ Ver. Code ☐☐☐ Check # __________

2012 AQS Paducah Quilt Show Sponsors

AQS presents the sponsors for the 28th Annual Quilt Show & Contest. Each category and event is sponsored by a company in the quilting industry. To open the show, company representatives present the cash awards at the Awards Presentation on Tuesday evening, April 24.

Best of Show .Janome America, Inc.
Hand Workmanship Award . . . . .American Quilter's Society
Machine Workmanship Award . . . . .BERNINA of America, Inc.
Longarm Machine Quilting Award . . . . . . .American Professional Quilting Systems
Best Wall Quilt Award. . . . . .Moda Fabrics
Wall Hand Workmanship Award . . . . .Coats & Clark
Wall Machine Workmanship Award . . . . . .Brother International Corporation
Wall Longarm Workmanship Award . . . . . .Handi Quilter
Best Miniature Quilt. . . . . .Benartex, Inc.
Bed Quilts
Hand Quilted . . . . .Superior Threads
Home Machine Quilted. . . . . .EZ Quilting by Wrights/Simplicity Creative Group
Longarm / Midarm Machine Quilted. . . .Hobbs Bonded Fibers
Group Quilt . . . . .Innova
Large Wall Quilts
Hand Quilted . . . . .Fairfield Processing Corporation
Home Machine Quilted. . . . . .Baby Lock USA
Longarm / Midarm Machine Quilted. . . .Robert Kaufman Co., Inc.
Pictorial Quilts. . . . . .Elna USA
1st Entry in AQS Quilt Contest . . . . . . .Morgan Quality Products
Small Wall Quilts
Hand Quilted . . . . .FreeSpirit/Westminster Fabrics
Home Machine Quilted. . . . . .Koala Cabinets
Longarm / Midarm Machine Quilted. . . .Hoffman California Fabrics
Pictorial Quilts. . . . . .Horn of America
1st Entry in AQS Quilt Contest . . . . . . .YLI Corporation
Miniature Quilts . . . . .Juki America, Inc.
Judges' Recognition . . . . .Tin Lizzie 18
Event Sponsors. . . . . .Baby Lock Building Quilts for Love, Ken's Sewing Center
General Sponsors . . . . .A1 Quilting Machines; ABM International; AccuQuilt; Amazing Designs; Gammill Quilting Systems; HQ Pro-Stitcher; Jenny Haskins Designs; Nolting; Pellon/Legacy; Quilt in a Day; Rotary Club of Paducah; Statler Stitcher; Timeless Treasures;
AQS Quilt Show Giveaway Gammill Quilting Systems; Tracey's Tables
Workshops . . . . .BERNINA of America; Inc., Elna USA; Handi Quilter; Janome America, Inc.,
The National Quilt Museum Workshop Series
. . . . .Flynn Quilt Frame Co.; Janome America, Inc.; Olfa Corporation
The National Quilt Museum New Quilts from an Old Favorite Contest: Baskets
Moda Fabrics; Janome America, Inc.
School Block Challenge . . . . .Moda Fabrics